Classics Alive!

Late Elementary to Early Intermediate Works by 12 Important Composers of Standard Teaching Literature

Compiled and Edited by

Jane Magrath

Classics Alive! Book 1 offers teachers and students a wide selection of literature to help pace musical and technical development evenly and with ease. The book presents standard teaching literature by 12 composers—familiar and not so familiar—who wrote exceptionally well for the late-elementary/early-intermediate student. All pieces are from levels 3 and 4, according to Jane Magrath's *The Pianist's Guide to Standard Teaching and Performance Literature* (from which the leveling chart on this page is taken).

Studying these works will give students a solid foundation in the best literature available at their level, and will prepare them to proceed to more advanced music. The pieces are easy to learn, rewarding to play and sound great! Enjoy!

Jane Magrath

Editorial note
Fingering throughout the book is editorial. Dynamics and articulation are editorial for Bach, Handel and Scarlatti. For the other composers, editorial markings and pedaling were added sparingly. All suggestions strive to steer the performer in the direction of the most stylistically appropriate performance possible.

Appreciation is extended to Morty and Iris Manus, E. L. Lancaster, and Kim Newman for their support.

Leveling of Literature—Reference Chart for Grading
Levels 1–10, Beginning to Early-Advanced Levels

Level 1   Bartók *Mikrokosmos*, Vol. 1

Level 2   Türk *Pieces for Beginners*

Level 3   Latour Sonatinas; Kabalevsky *Pieces for Young People*, Op. 39

Level 4   *Anna Magdalena Bach Notebook;* Gurlitt *Album for the Young*, Op. 140; Tchaikovsky *Album for the Young*, Op. 39

Level 5   *Anna Magdalena Bach Notebook;* Sonatinas by Attwood, Lynes; Menotti *Poemetti*

Level 6   Clementi *Sonatinas*, Op. 36; Burgmüller *25 Progressive Pieces*, Op. 100

Level 7   Kuhlau and Diabelli Sonatinas; Bach easier *Two-Part Inventions;* Bach *Little Preludes;* Dello Joio *Lyric Pieces for the Young*

Level 8   Moderately difficult Bach *Two-Part Inventions;* Beethoven easier variations sets; Field Nocturnes; Schumann *Album Leaves*, Op. 124; Schubert Waltzes; Turina *Miniatures*

Level 9   Easier Bach *Three-Part Inventions;* easiest Haydn Sonata movements; easiest Mendelssohn *Songs Without Words;* easiest Chopin Mazurkas

Level 10   Bach *Three-Part Inventions;* easiest Chopin Nocturnes; Beethoven *Sonatas*, Op. 49, 79; Mozart *Sonata*, K. 283; Muczynski *Preludes*

Table of Contents

Suggested Order of Study

Air in F Major

BWV Anh. 131

from the *Notebook for Anna Magdalena* (1725)

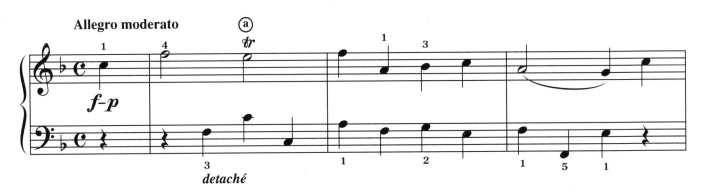

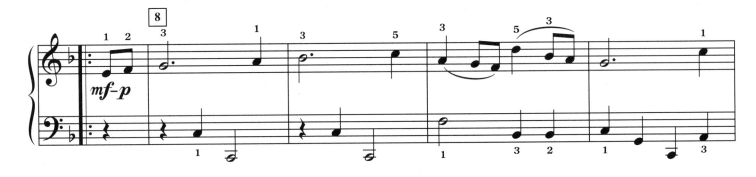

ⓑ An embellishment may be added here:

Minuet in G Major

from *Suite in G Minor,* BWV 822

Johann Sebastian Bach

Minuet in G Major

BWV Anh. 116

from the *Notebook for Anna Magdalena* (1725)

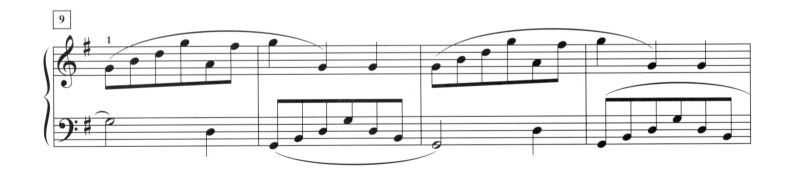

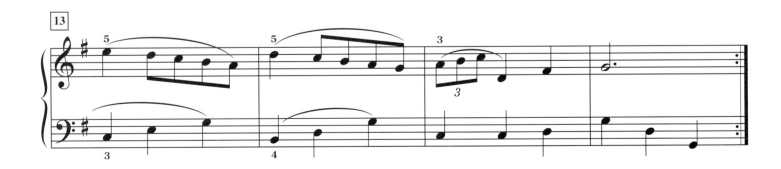

(a) Most modern editions have D♯ here. The sharp does not appear in the original manuscript.

Musette in D Major

BWV Anh. 126

from the *Notebook for Anna Magdalena* (1725)

Moderato

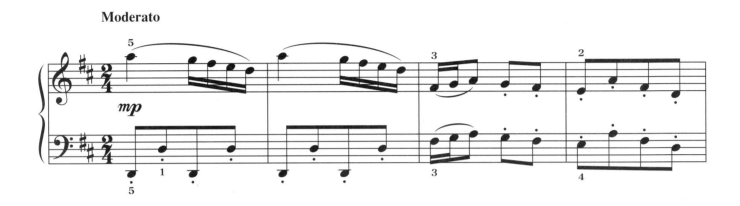

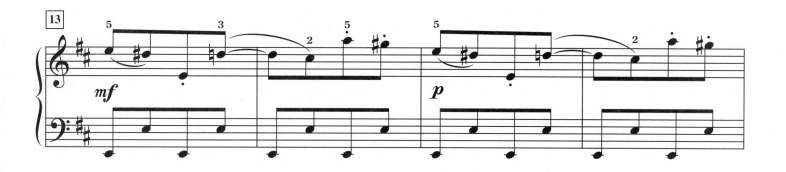

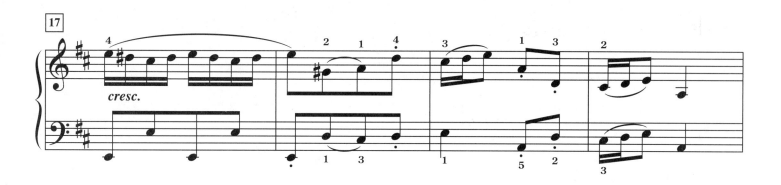

Musette in G Major

from *English Suite in G Minor*, BWV 808

Johann Sebastian Bach

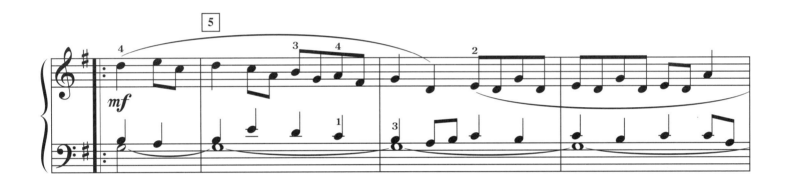

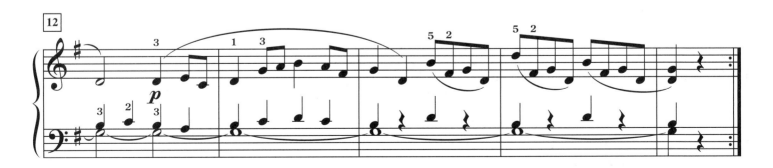

ⓐ Restrike the LH G.

Prelude in C Major

BWV 939

Johann Sebastian Bach

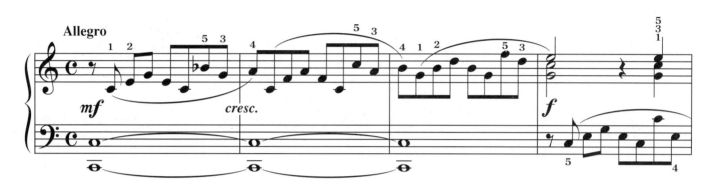

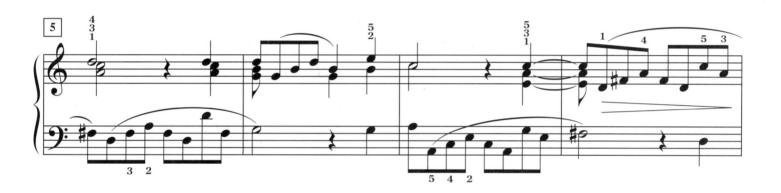

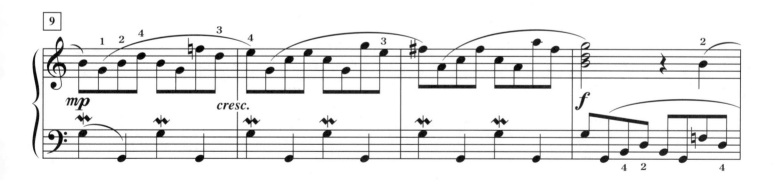

Passepied in C Major

George Frideric Handel

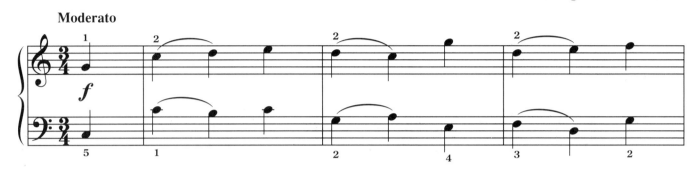

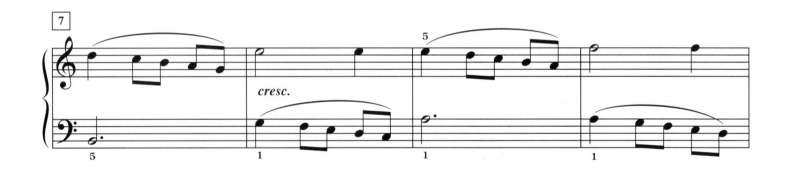

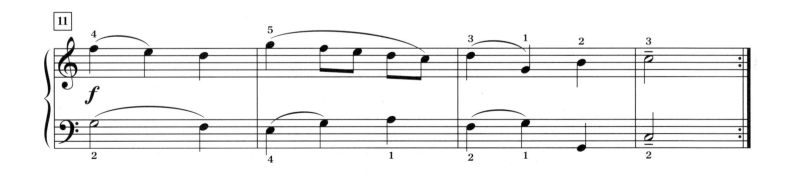

Minuet in B Minor

George Frideric Handel

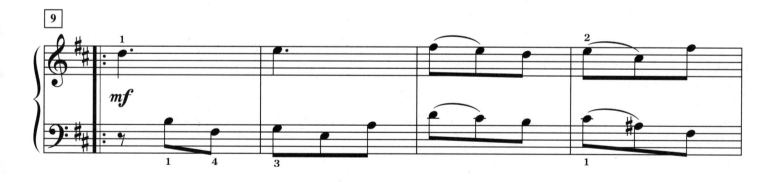

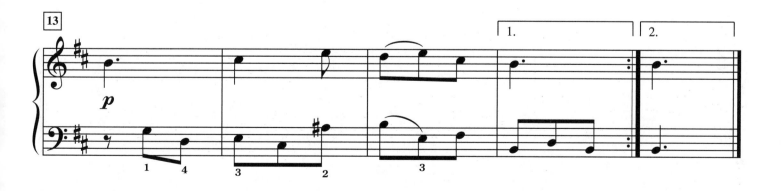

Minuet in F Major

George Frideric Handel

Minuet in B-flat Major

George Frideric Handel

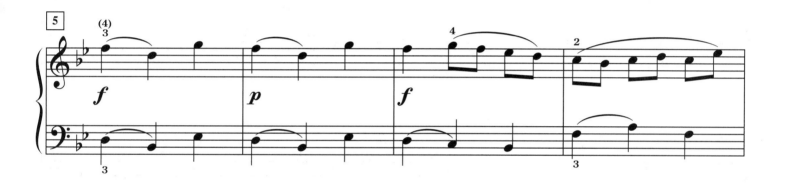

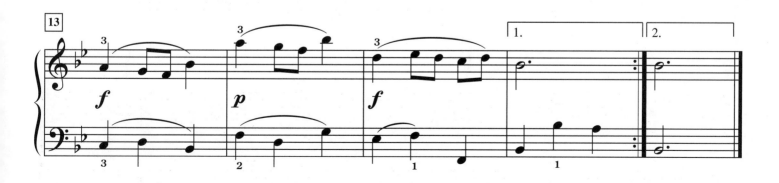

Minuet in G Major

George Frideric Handel

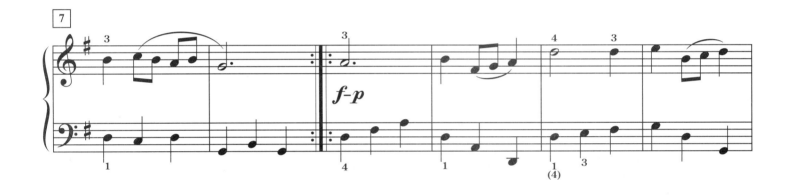

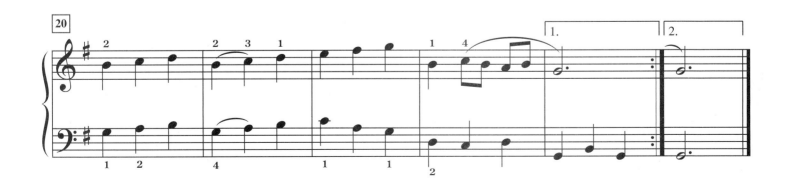

Air in B-flat Major

George Frideric Handel

Gavotte in G Major

George Frideric Handel

Sonata in C Major

K. 73b, L. 217

Domenico Scarlatti

Sonata in D Minor

K. 32, L. 423

Domenico Scarlatti

ⓐ Arpeggiate the left-hand chords in measures 1, 3, 5, 9, 11, 17 and 21 from the lowest note:

Minuet in F Major
K. 2

Wolfgang Amadeus Mozart

Tempo di menuetto

Minuet in C Major
K. 6

Wolfgang Amadeus Mozart

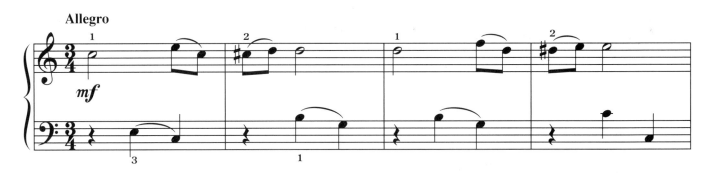

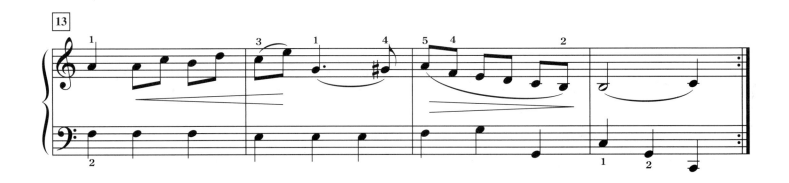

Allegro in B-flat Major

K. 3

Wolfgang Amadeus Mozart

Minuet and Trio in G Major
K. 1

Wolfgang Amadeus Mozart

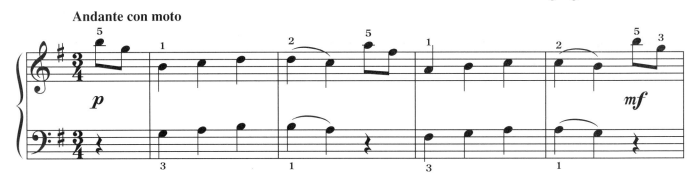

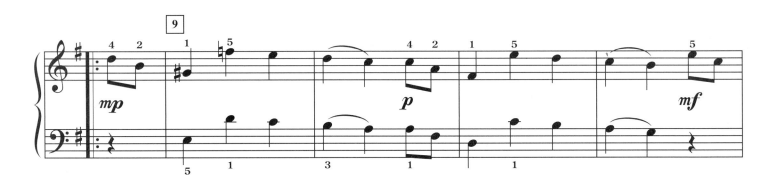

TRIO

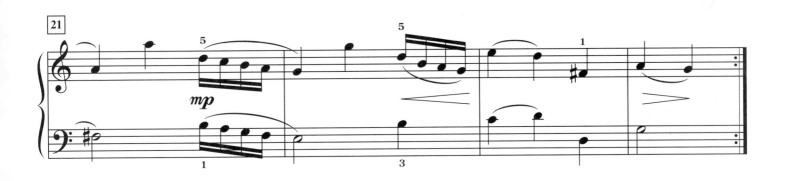

D.C. al Fine

Minuet in A-flat Major

K. 15ff

Wolfgang Amadeus Mozart

Tempo di menuetto

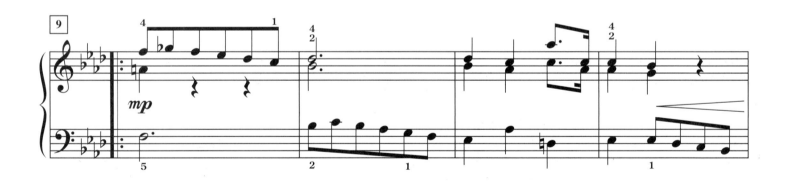

Minuet in E-flat Major
K. 15qq

Wolfgang Amadeus Mozart

German Dance in E Major

Hob. IX:22/9

Franz Joseph Haydn

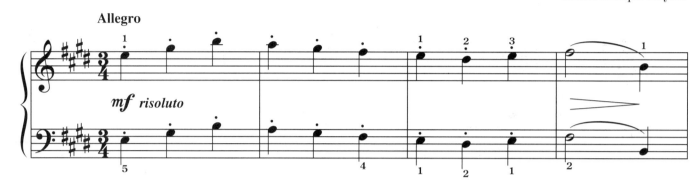

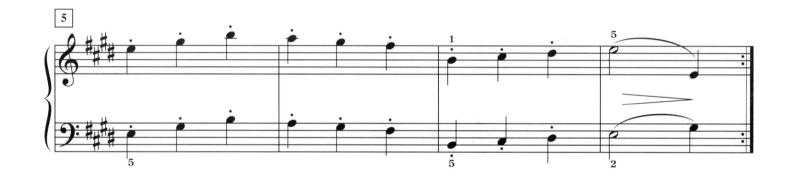

German Dance in D Major

Hob. IX:22/2

Franz Joseph Haydn

ⓐ   Play the D on the beat.

Country Dance in D Major

Hob. XXXIc:17b

Franz Joseph Haydn

Minuet in A Major

Hob. IX:10/21

Franz Joseph Haydn

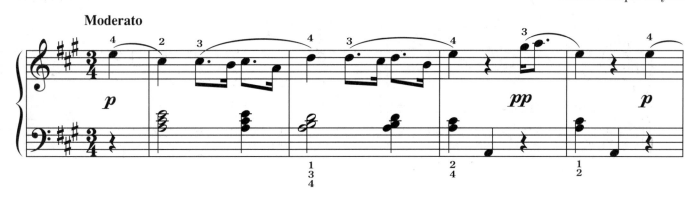

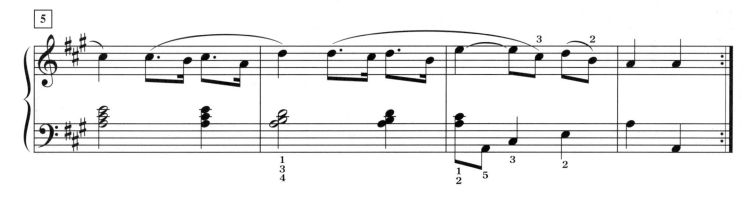

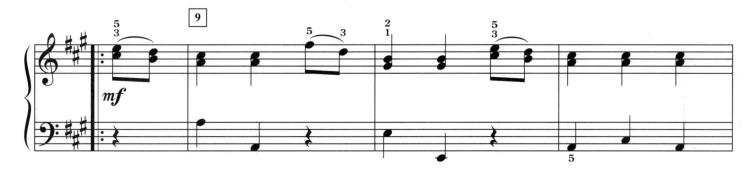

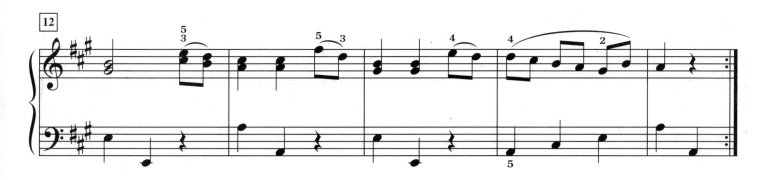

Minuet in A Major

Hob. IX:8/6

Franz Joseph Haydn

Minuet in B-flat Major

Hob. IX:8/3

Franz Joseph Haydn

German Dance in C Major

WoO 8, No. 1

Ludwig van Beethoven

Ländler in D Major

WoO 15, No. 1

Ludwig van Beethoven

(a) Ländler is the German word for country dance.

Romanze from Sonatina in G Major

Anh. 5, No. 1

Ludwig van Beethoven

(a) Play the B on the beat, almost simultaneously with the A:

Ländler in D Major

WoO 15, No. 2

Ludwig van Beethoven

Écossaise in E-flat Major
WoO 86

Ludwig van Beethoven

Ländler in D Major

WoO 11, No. 3

Ludwig van Beethoven

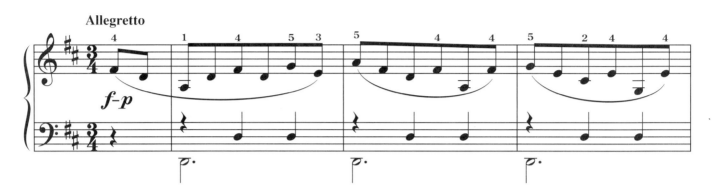

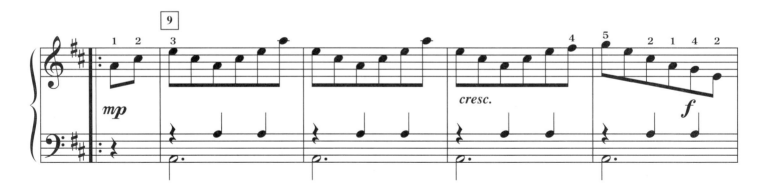

Humming Song

Op. 68, No. 3

Robert Schumann

A Little Piece
Op. 68, No. 5

Robert Schumann

Melody
Op. 68, No. 1

Robert Schumann

Little Study
Op. 68, No.14

Robert Schumann

Leise und sehr egal zu spielen (Lightly and very evenly)

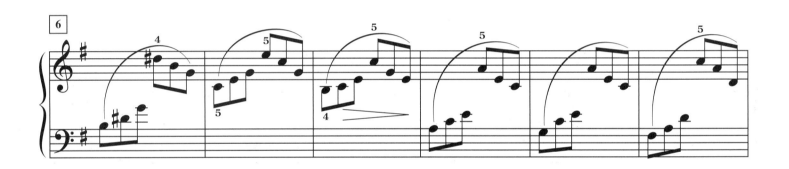

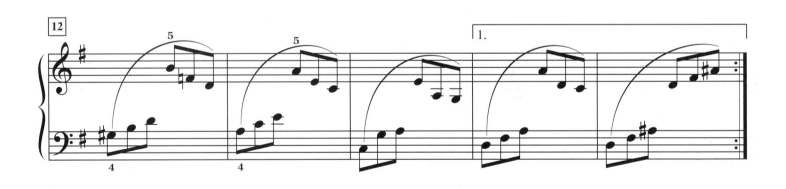

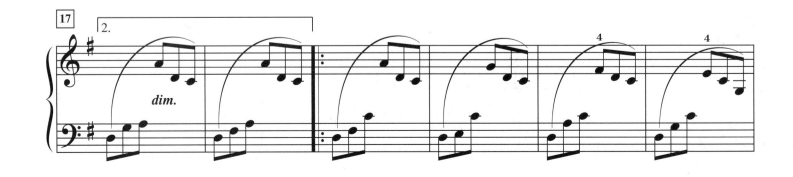

The Reaper's Song
Op. 68, No. 18

Robert Schumann

Nicht sehr schnell (Not very fast)

Sicilienne
Op. 68, No. 11

Robert Schumann

Schalkhaft (**Mischievously**)

Fine

Schnell (Fast)

D.C. al Fine without repetitions

First Loss

Op. 68, No. 16

Robert Schumann

Sincerity
Op. 100, No. 1

Johann Friedrich Burgmüller

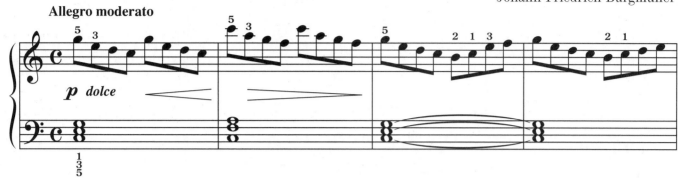

Allegro moderato

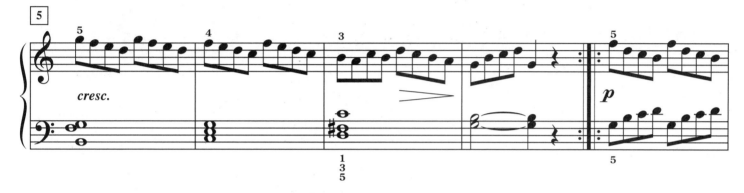

Pastorale
Op. 100, No. 3

Johann Friedrich Burgmüller

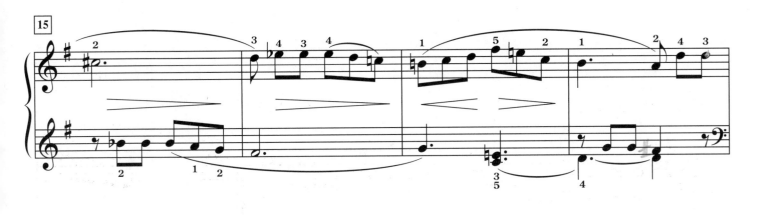

Arabesque
Op. 100, No. 2

Johann Friedrich Burgmüller

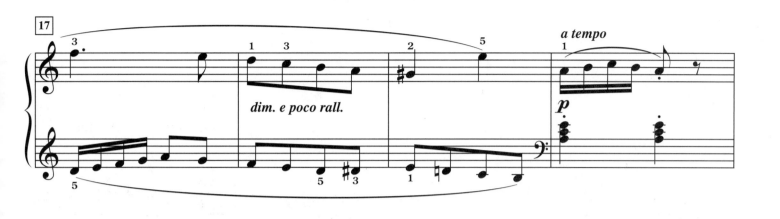

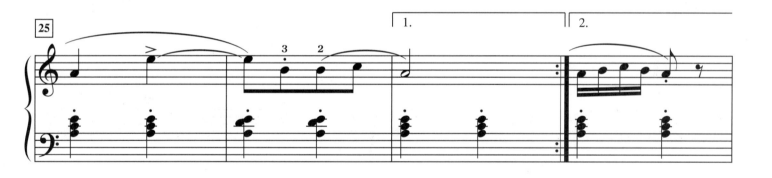

Innocence
Op. 100, No. 5

Johann Friedrich Burgmüller

Ballade
Op. 100, No. 15

Johann Friedrich Burgmüller

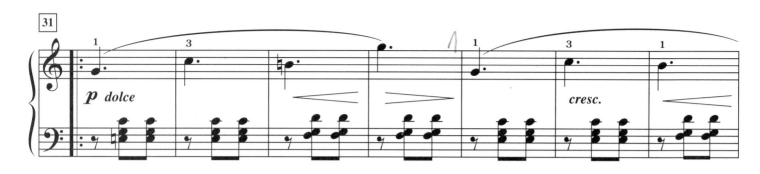

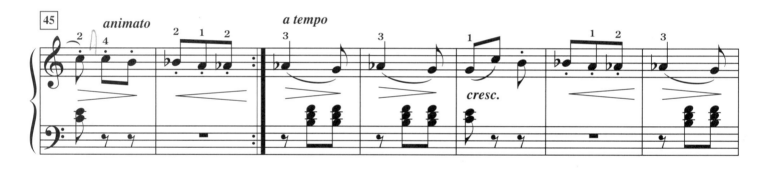

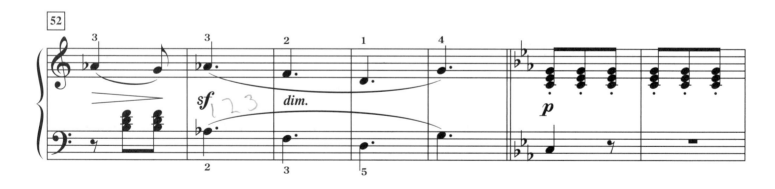

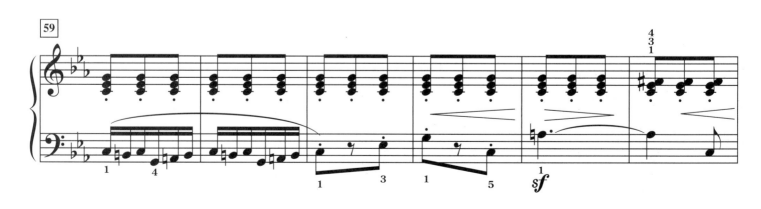

The Clear Stream

Op. 100, No. 7

Johann Friedrich Burgmüller

Little Flower (Wild Mignonette)

Op. 205, No. 1

The individual flower names did not originate with Gurlitt,
but rather with the 1936 Augener edition of these pieces.
Performers may want to consider them in the interpretations.

The *Wild Mignonette* is a tall flowering plant with small, yellow-green flowers.

Cornelius Gurlitt

Little Flower (Lady's Smock)

Op. 205, No. 3

Lady's Smock grows in small bunches of stalks with dark green leaves
and white flowers. Its name comes from the way the flowers resemble
smocks laid out by Elizabethan maidens to dry in the sun.

Cornelius Gurlitt

Little Flower (Rose Rock)

Op. 205, No. 8

Rose Rock is a wildflower with five yellow or white petals.
Its scent is said to be calming.

Cornelius Gurlitt

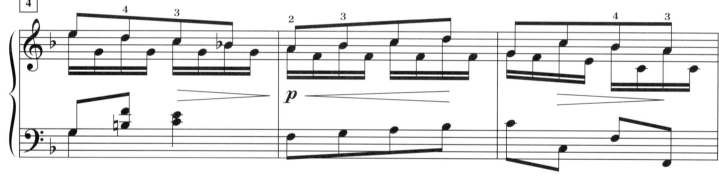

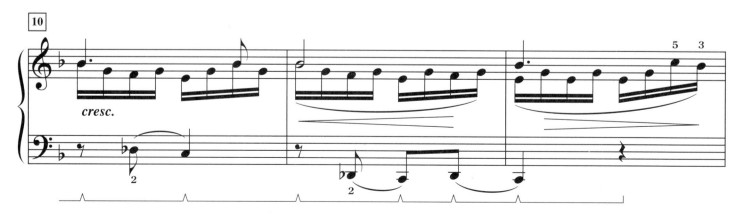

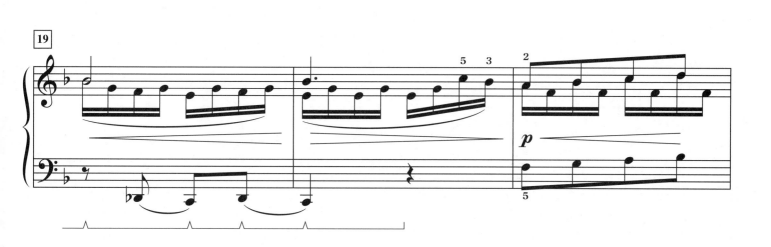

Little Flower (Heather)
Op. 205, No. 6

Heather ranges in size and shape from
ground cover to upright trees, with flowers
of white, pink, mauve and crimson.

Cornelius Gurlitt

Little Flower (Harebell)

Op. 205, No. 2

The *Harebell* plant features deep blue bell-shaped flowers.

Cornelius Gurlitt

Etude in D Major
Op. 141, No. 17

Cornelius Gurlitt

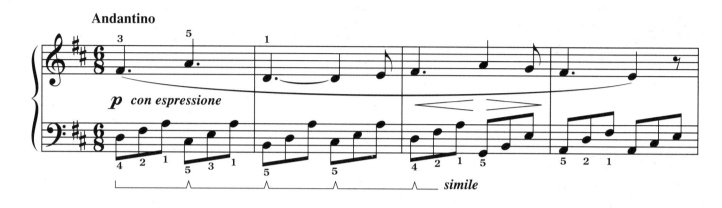

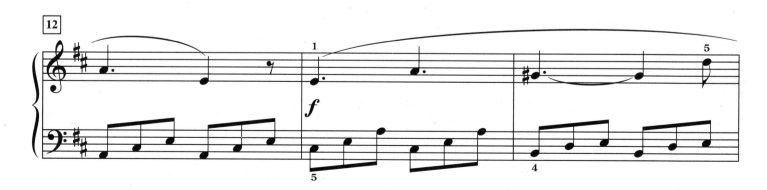

Etude in E Minor

Op. 141, No. 23

Cornelius Gurlitt

Moderato

p **espressivo e tenuto il canto** (a)

cresc.   *decresc.*   *poco riten.*

a tempo

pp   *simile*

cresc.

(a) Expressively; bring out the melody.

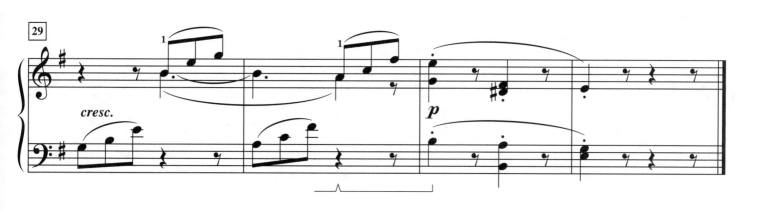

A Magic Dance

(No. 5 from *For Children*, Book 1)

Béla Bartók

Poco allegretto

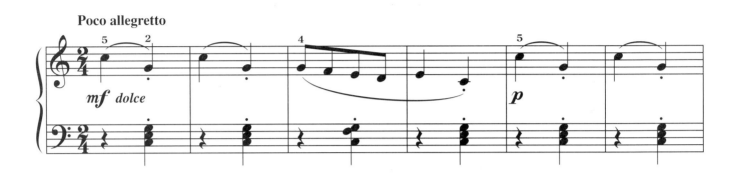

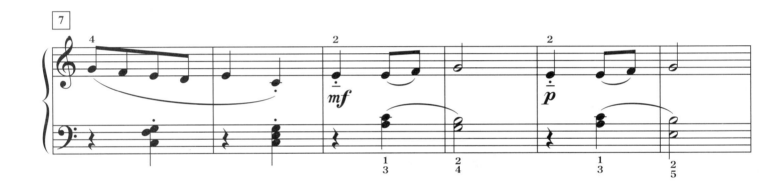

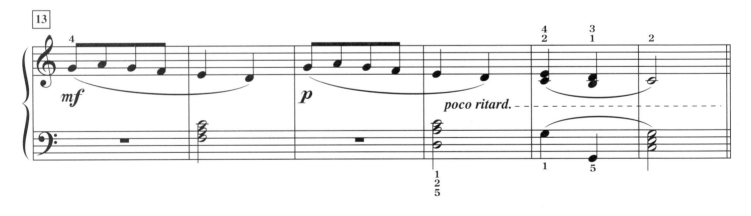

Poco più vivo

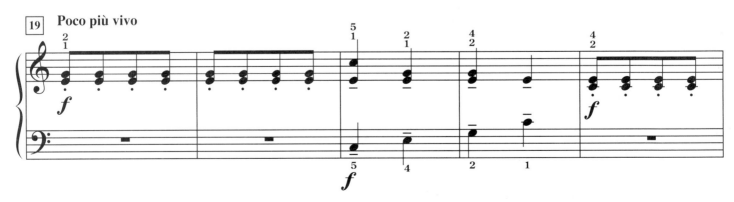

Circle Dance

(No. 8 from *For Children*, Book 1)

Béla Bartók

Folk Tune

(No. 2 from *For Children*, Book 1)

Béla Bartók

Andante

(No. 3 from *For Children*, Book 1)

Béla Bartók

Minuet
from *First Term at the Piano*

Béla Bartók

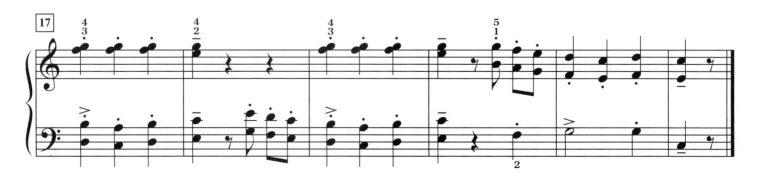

Vagabond

(No. 7 from *For Children*, Book 2)

Béla Bartók

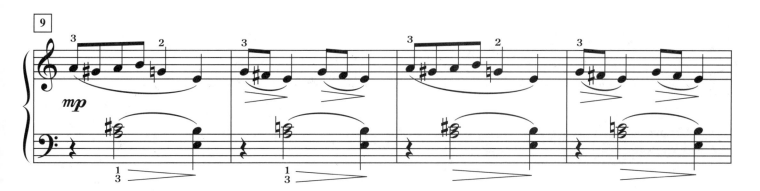

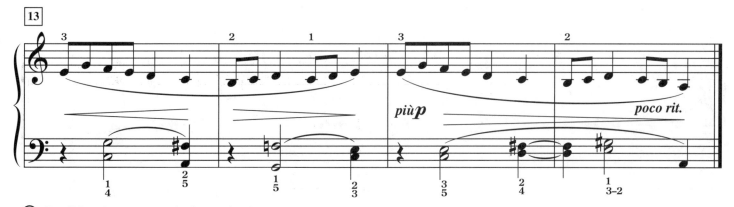

ⓐ Small hands may omit the lower A.

Chinese Figurine

(No. 13 from *Christmas Gifts*)

Vladimir Rebikov

Statuette

(No. 11 from *Christmas Gifts*)

Vladimir Rebikov

Russian Doll

(No. 5 from *Christmas Gifts*)

Vladimir Rebikov

Dance of the Gnomes

(No. 2 from *Christmas Gifts*)

Vladimir Rebikov

The Witch in the Forest

Op. 31, No. 9

Vladimir Rebikov

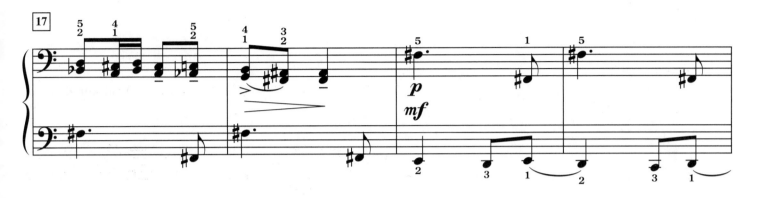

Pastoral Scene

Op. 10, No. 1

Vladimir Rebikov

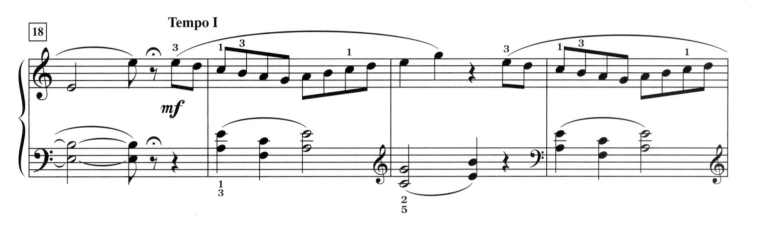

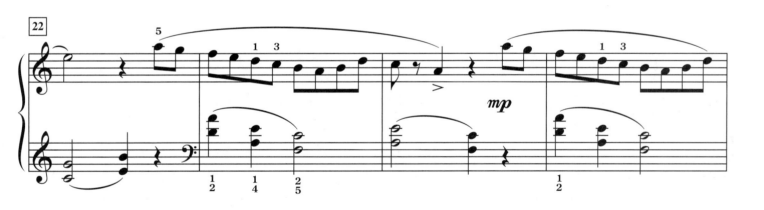

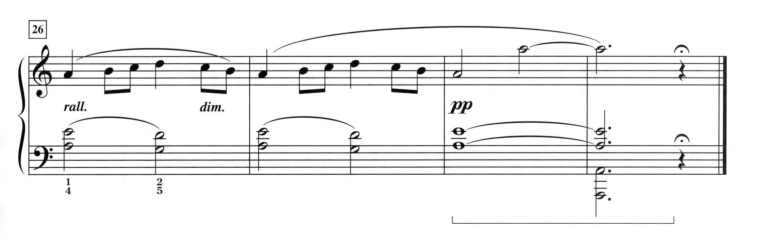

Gather Around the Christmas Tree

(No. 1 from *Christmas Gifts*)

Vladimir Rebikov

Petite Pièce
Op. 6, No. 2

Alexander Goedicke

Moderato

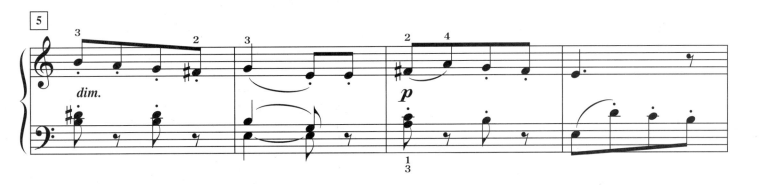

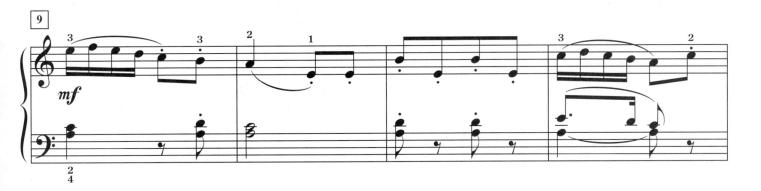

Petite Pièce

Op. 6, No. 1

Alexander Goedicke

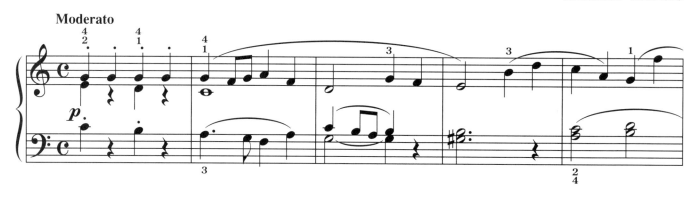

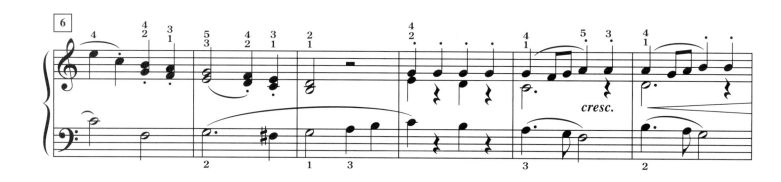

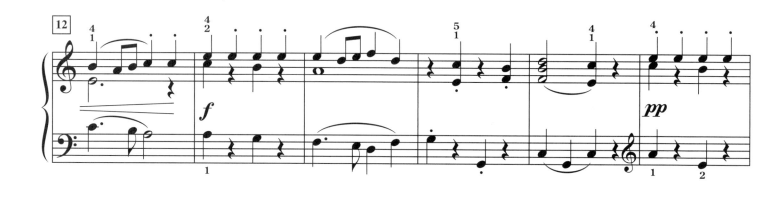

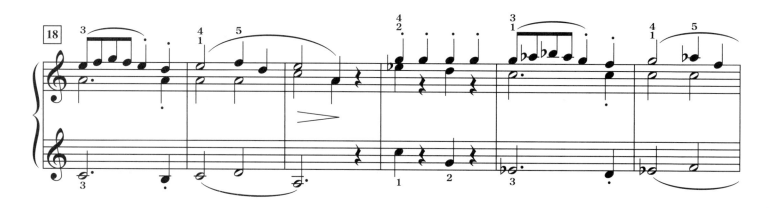

Petite Pièce
Op. 6, No. 5

Alexander Goedicke

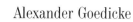

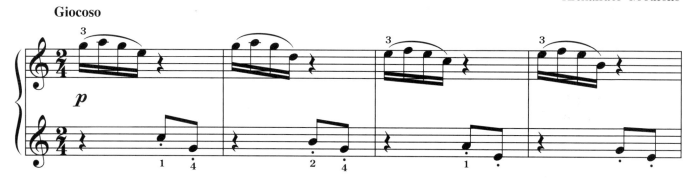

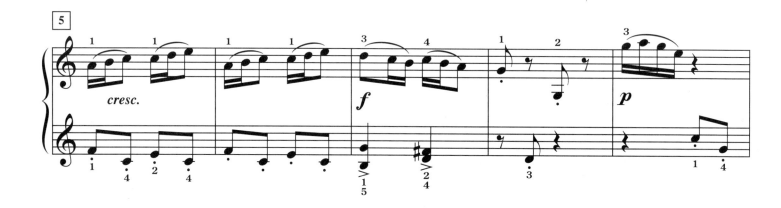

Petite Pièce
Op. 6, No. 9

Alexander Goedicke

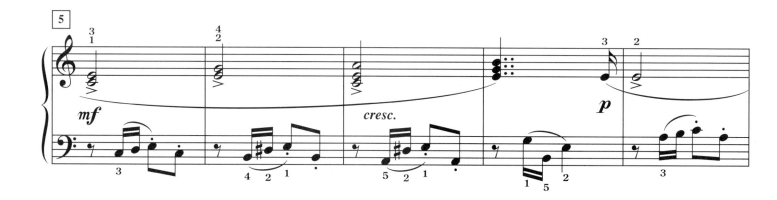

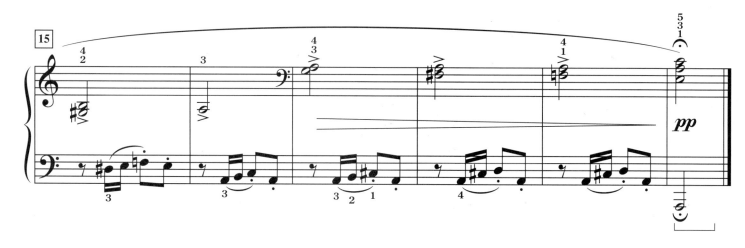

Petite Pièce

Op. 6, No. 10

Alexander Goedicke

Composer Biographies

Johann Sebastian Bach (1685–1750, Germany) was a composer and organist. Born in Eisenach, Germany, he studied several musical disciplines as a boy, including violin, harpsichord, clavichord, organ and singing. He composed many keyboard works, including the 48 Preludes and Fugues from the *Well-Tempered Clavier* Books 1 and 2, 6 *French Suites*, 6 *English Suites* and 6 *Partitas* (all sets of dances), *Inventions* for two and three voices, and numerous other miscellaneous keyboard works. The *Notebook for Anna Magdalena Bach* from 1725 was probably a gift from the composer to his wife Anna Magdalena; it contained pieces intended for the musical education of their children.

George Frideric Handel (1685–1759, England, born Germany) enjoyed fame as a performer and improviser on the harpsichord and organ. His keyboard works were composed during the first part of his creative life. Later in his life at the age of 53 he turned his attention toward composing sacred oratorios of which *Messiah*, composed in slightly under three weeks, is the greatest.

Domenico Scarlatti (1685–1757, Spain, born Italy), born in the same year as Handel and Bach, lived most of his life in Portugal and Spain. From 1720 to 1725 Scarlatti was court harpsichordist to the King of Portugal and teacher of his daughter Princess Maria Barbara, remaining her teacher even after she moved to Madrid in 1727. Her skill as a performer was likely the inspiration for his over 500 single-movement keyboard sonatas, which were innovative in the use of unusual keyboard techniques, such as crossed hands and rapid repeated notes.

Wolfgang Amadeus Mozart (1756–1791, Austria) composed in many musical mediums with equal brilliance, and was one of the greatest child prodigies ever.

Mozart began to compose at the age of five by writing pieces for keyboard, and from then on composed quickly and easily. At the age of nine he composed his first choral piece, and composed his first opera at age 12.

Franz Joseph Haydn (1732–1809, Austria) was 24 years older than Mozart, yet outlived him by 18 years. Haydn produced an enormous output of music, including 47 keyboard sonatas and 104 symphonies. For nearly 50 years he was in the service of Prince Esterházy, a wealthy Hungarian nobleman. He was the supreme example of a royal court musician, with a full orchestra of musicians to try out his musical ideas. He was called "Papa Haydn" by his friends in appreciation of his likable personality and good sense of humor.

Ludwig van Beethoven (1770–1827, Germany) was born in Bonn and grew up in a musical home. He began piano study at a young age and was a keyboard virtuoso by the time he had reached adulthood; at one point he was known as the greatest pianist of his time. The sense of humor in his music was more offbeat than the cheerful humor of Haydn. Throughout his music one finds sudden shifts in emotion and numerous surprises through changes of rhythm, key and dynamics.

Robert Schumann (1810–1856, Germany), born in Zwickau, began piano lessons at the age of six. His piano works primarily consist of sets of short pieces with descriptive titles—character pieces. Robert fell in love with, and eventually married Clara Wieck, a concert pianist and daughter of his piano teacher, who did not approve of the courtship. Schumann wrote secret messages to Clara through motives in his compositions.

Johann Friedrich Burgmüller (1806–1876, Germany, died France), born in Regensburg, was a popular pianist in the nineteenth century, especially in the Paris salons where his light and intimate style of playing won him many admirers. His ability to improvise tuneful selections is reflected in the hundreds of teaching pieces he wrote, many of which are still popular. His best known piano collection is the set of *Twenty-five Progressive Etudes*, Op. 100.

Cornelius Gurlitt (1820–1902, Germany) belonged to the circle of friends of Schumann and Brahms. As an instructor at the Hamburg School of Music, Gurlitt composed many studies for young musicians and amateurs. His music is in the romantic style, somewhat similar to that of Schumann.

Béla Bartók (1881–1945, Hungary) was both a concert pianist and composer. He traveled throughout Rumania and Slovakia listening to and recording folks songs of the people of those regions. Bartók's music often uses Hungarian and other folk tunes as its basis. He wrote numerous piano works for beginners including *Mikrokosmos* and *For Children*, Books 1 and 2.

Vladimir Rebikov (1866–1920, Russia) studied at the Moscow Conservatory in Russia, and lived in Moscow most of his life. His early works were more conservative and romantic in nature, but later in life he moved toward a more modern style, employing the whole tone scale, augmented triads, consecutive fourths and fifths and unresolved dissonances

Alexander Goedicke (1877–1957, Russia) was a Russian pianist and composer who came from a musical family. Like Rebikov, he studied piano at the Moscow Conservatory where he also studied composition. Goedicke won the Rubinstein Prize for Composition at the age of 23. Later he became professor of piano at the Moscow Conservatory where he also taught organ.